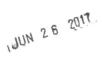
TEEN 973.933 R436d
Donald Trump :45th US
 president /
Reston, Dominick,

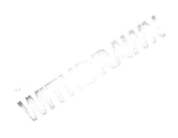

Donald Trump: 45th US President

Dominick Reston

ReferencePoint
Press®

San Diego, CA

About the Author
Dominick Reston lives in Southern California and writes nonfiction for both adults and young adults.

© 2018 ReferencePoint Press, Inc.
Printed in the United States

For more information, contact:
ReferencePoint Press, Inc.
PO Box 27779
San Diego, CA 92198
www.ReferencePointPress.com

LIBRARY OF CONGRESS CATALOGING-IN-PUBLICATION DATA

Name: Reston, Dominick–author.
Title: Donald Trump: 45th US President/by Dominick Reston.
Description: San Diego, CA: ReferencePoint Press, 2017. | Includes
   bibliographical references and index. | Audience: Grade 9 to 12.
Identifiers: LCCN 2017001820 (print) | LCCN 2017002779 (ebook) | ISBN
   9781682822951 (hardback) | ISBN 9781682822968 (eBook)
Subjects: LCSH: Trump, Donald, 1946– | Presidents—United
   States—Election—2016. | Presidents—United States—Biography. | United
   States—Politics and government—2009–
Classification: LCC E911 .K35 2017 (print) | LCC E911 (ebook) | DDC
   973.933092 [B] —dc23
LC record available at https://lccn.loc.gov/2017001820

Contents

Introduction

A Bet That Paid Off

On June 16, 2015, reporters, television cameras, and several hundred people gathered in the lobby of Trump Tower, a fifty-eight-story skyscraper in Manhattan. A podium on a stage held a banner with the slogan "Make America Great Again!" All heads turned as sixty-nine-year-old Donald John Trump made a grand entrance, riding down a multistory escalator with his wife, Melania. Trump biographer Gwenda Blair describes the scene: "Gazing out, they seemed for a moment like a royal couple viewing subjects from the balcony of the palace."[1] Trump flashed two thumbs up and took his place on the stage to proclaim his intention to campaign for the Republican nomination for president.

Unlike the other politicians hoping to be elected president in November 2016, Trump was a billionaire and international celebrity who had been in the public eye for decades. Trump was known as a negotiator, salesman, television personality, and builder of glittering skyscrapers. He was involved in high-end real estate transactions, casinos, golf courses, beauty pageants, and the reality show *The Apprentice*. Trump's name was spelled out in shiny gold letters on luxury skyscrapers, golf courses, resorts, and other properties throughout the world.

Negative Images

Many people associated the Trump name with success, wealth, and fame. But most pundits and political analysts who heard Trump's presidential announcement speech did not believe he would ever be elected president. Trump did not possess the smooth personality and political skills of a typical presidential candidate. He was notorious for giving speeches that wandered from topic to topic. He made outrageous statements on Twitter and supported shadowy conspiracy theories, including one that claimed that President Barack Obama was born in Kenya. Moreover, there was a widespread belief that presidential candidates needed to present an optimistic view of the United States and provide a positive vision of the future. In contrast, Trump focused on negative images. "Our country is in serious trouble," he said in his presidential campaign announcement speech. "We don't have victories anymore. We used to have victories, but we don't have them." In that same speech Trump went on to say that the Mexican people were laughing at American stupidity: "When Mexico sends its people, they're not sending their best. . . . They're bringing drugs. They're bringing crime. They're rapists. And some, I assume, are good people." He went on to say that "the American dream is dead" and that only he could restore it.[2]

Trump's speech set off a media firestorm. Democrats and Republicans appeared on cable television news shows and social media websites to condemn Trump's biased statements. Respected political analysts pointed out that Trump was not popular enough to win the White House; a Gallup poll taken after the speech showed that only 31 percent of potential voters had a favorable view of Trump. No candidate had ever won a national race with such a low approval rating. As journalist Chris Cillizza wrote, "You cannot and do not win anything when your numbers look like Trump's. I can't say it any more clearly than that."[3]

> "Our country is in serious trouble. We don't have victories anymore. We used to have victories, but we don't have them."[2]
>
> —Donald Trump

Defying the Odds

But after the presidential primary season began in February 2016, Trump accomplished something that almost no one thought was possible. He beat sixteen contenders in the Republican presidential primaries and caucuses to win the nomination. And on November 8, 2016, he again defied the odds (and the polls and pundits) by winning enough electoral votes to defeat Hillary Clinton, the Democratic nominee.

Millions of people worldwide were stunned by Trump's victory. He had broken all the traditional rules of a political campaign for president: he had never run for office or served in the military. He painted life in the United States in apocalyptic terms, insulted and demeaned his rivals, and threatened to sue journalists and other critics. During the campaign Trump was accused of inciting hostility against women, immigrants, Muslims, African Americans, Jews, and even military veterans. According to various fact-checking websites, Trump's speeches and public statements often fell short of the truth. (In December 2016, for instance, the nonpartisan fact-checking website PolitiFact said that 78 percent of Trump's statements during the campaign were false or mostly false. For Clinton, that number was 18 percent.) But Trump understood that his outrageous comments—and his late-night Twitter storms—attracted nonstop attention from the press. The endless free publicity in the media helped energize his followers.

Although some of Trump's supporters did not agree with his more shocking statements, they appreciated his economic message. Trump spoke out against Wall Street brokers, bankers, and corporations; he said they had abandoned American workers by taking their operations overseas. He promised to bring back millions of lost jobs. He criticized the elite of both political parties, which broadened his appeal to white working-class voters who felt that they had been left behind economically.

Trump's campaign rallies were more like rock concerts than political gatherings. Ecstatic crowds donned matching T-shirts and baseball caps. They cheered wildly as the candidate hurled insults before promis-

> "For all of [Trump's] faults . . . he made a daring bet that paid off. He told a story that half of Americans wanted to hear."[4]
>
> —Viet Thanh Nguyen, literary critic

ing them a better, brighter future. As literary critic Viet Thanh Nguyen puts it, "For all of [Trump's] faults, and there are many, he made a daring bet that paid off. He told a story that half of Americans wanted to hear."[4] And for that he was rewarded with arguably the most influential job in the world. On January 20, 2017, Donald Trump became the forty-fifth president of the United States.

Chapter 1

Born Into a Wealthy Family

When Donald John Trump was born on June 14, 1946, in Queens, New York, his family had been in the real estate business for two generations. Donald's grandfather Friedrich Trump, who was born in the small town of Kallstadt, Germany, grew wealthy after moving to the United States in 1885 at the age of sixteen. Donald's father, Fred Trump, was a real estate developer who constructed thousands of row houses and almost twenty-five thousand apartment units in the New York City boroughs of Brooklyn and Queens.

The Trump family fortune can be traced to Donald's grandfather Friedrich, who opened a restaurant, saloon, and brothel in the Klondike region of the Yukon in Canada in 1896 during the gold rush. In 1902 Friedrich married Elizabeth Christ, a native of Kallstadt. The couple moved to Queens, where Donald Trump's father, Frederick "Fred" Christ Trump, was born in 1905. By 1915 the population of Queens was growing quickly, which inspired Friedrich to invest his savings in the real estate market. He bought five vacant lots and set up a mortgage company to loan money to people who wished to buy houses.

In 1918 an influenza pandemic killed somewhere between 20 million and 40 million people worldwide. Forty-nine-year-old Friedrich Trump was among the victims. At the time of his death Friedrich was worth around $32,000. This was a substantial sum of money during this era when the average industrial worker made $25 a week and a three-bedroom home in Queens sold for $3,000.

Elizabeth Trump & Son

After Friedrich's death his wife, Elizabeth, took over the family's real estate business. Although Fred Trump was only thirteen years old, he had developed a strong interest in the building trades. This prompted his mother to form a new real estate company that she called Elizabeth Trump & Son. Fred took an active role and built and sold his first home when he was only seventeen. He used the profits to buy, build, and sell a number of homes, increasing his wealth as the population of Queens more than doubled between 1920 and 1930. Many years later,

> "My dad, Fred Trump . . . was a guy most comfortable in the company of bricklayers, carpenters, and electricians."[5]
>
> — Donald Trump

Donald described his father this way: "My dad, Fred Trump, was the smartest and hardest working man I ever knew. . . . He was a guy most comfortable in the company of bricklayers, carpenters, and electricians and I have a lot of that in me also."[5]

In 1935, thirty-year-old Fred Trump met Mary Anne MacLeod at a party in Queens. MacLeod, who was from a small village in the Outer Hebrides in the far north of Scotland, was twenty-three years old and working as a maid. Trump and MacLeod fell in love and were married in January 1936. In 1937 Mary gave birth to their first child, Maryanne, followed by Frederick Jr. in 1938.

Donald Trump's father, Frederick "Fred" Trump (pictured in 1987), amassed a fortune in real estate. He developed sales techniques that were considered both brash and bold.

During this period Fred came up with a brash, bold sales technique that was unusual for the era. In July 1939 he launched a home marketing event called the Trump Boat Show using a 65-foot (20 m) yacht. The ship sailed past hundreds of thousands of Coney Island sunbathers on a sweltering Sunday while recordings of "God Bless America" and "The Star Spangled Banner" blared from the deck. Fifty-foot (15 m) banners that promoted Trump homes fluttered on the side of the yacht. Fred generated further excitement by disbursing thousands of swordfish-shaped balloons with coupons for a $250 discount toward the purchase of a Trump home. This caused near riots as people pushed and shoved one another to grab the coupons. As journalist Jason Horowitz observed in 2016, "As a salesman, competitor . . . and, above all, as a showboating self-promoter, Fred Trump was the Donald Trump of his day."[6]

> "[Donald] would sit with his arms folded, with this look on his face—I would use the word *surly*—almost daring you to say one thing or another that didn't settle with him."[7]
>
> — Ann Trees, grade school teacher

A Surly Student

Fred and Mary Trump had another daughter, Elizabeth, in 1942. By the time Donald was born in 1946, Fred was one of the richest men in the United States. He built a twenty-three-room mansion in a wealthy Queens enclave called Jamaica Estates in 1948. Donald's younger brother, Robert, was born around this time.

The Trump residence stood out even in Jamaica Estates, where homes owned by doctors, lawyers, and powerful politicians were surrounded by giant oak trees and huge lawns. The Trump home, perched on a hill, featured stately white columns like those found on southern plantations. And unlike most of their neighbors, the Trumps had a cook, a maid, and a chauffeur; a Cadillac limousine with the license plate bearing Fred's initials, FCT, was often parked in the driveway.

When Donald was five he attended kindergarten at the private Kew-Forest School. Male students at Kew-Forest were required to wear suits and ties. Strict rules required them to rise and stand when their teachers entered the classroom. Despite the rules at school, Donald was becoming an unruly boy; he threw rocks at the children next door and threatened to call the police when their ball accidentally bounced into his yard. At Kew-Forest, Donald was called "Donny," "the Trumpet," and "Flat Top" for his striking blond pompadour. He made himself the center of attention, cracking jokes, interrupting his teachers, and throwing spitballs. His teachers quickly learned that he was headstrong and determined. In his 1987 best seller, *Trump: The Art of the Deal,* Trump wrote that in second grade he punched his music teacher, giving him a black eye because he did not think he knew anything about music. Another teacher, Ann Trees, described Donald: "He would sit with his arms folded, with

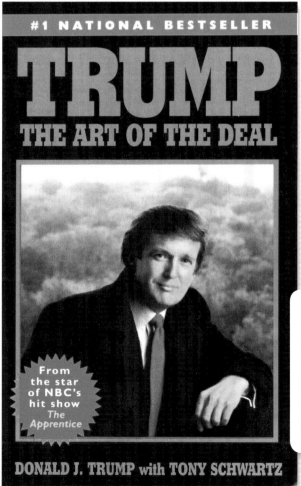

Published in 1987, Donald Trump's book *Trump: The Art of the Deal* sold more than 1 million copies and was on the *New York Times* best seller list for fifty-one weeks. The book details Trump's business philosophy and provides insight into his life at that time.

this look on his face—I would use the word *surly*—almost daring you to say one thing or another that wouldn't settle with him."[7]

Donald was sent to detention so many times that other students began referring to that form of punishment as the DTs, or Donald Trumps. In his book Trump writes, "Even early on I had a tendency to stand up and make my opinions known in a very forceful way. . . . I was mostly interested in creating mischief, because for some reason, I liked to stir things up and I liked to test people. . . . It wasn't malicious so much as it was aggressive."[8]

Learning Discipline

It might have been Fred who encouraged Donald's rebellious behavior; he always told his son that he was a king and needed to be a killer to be successful. However, when Donald was thirteen his life changed drastically after he defied his father's orders. Donald took to riding the subway into Manhattan with a friend to visit Times Square. Fred Trump believed this was a dangerous activity and had forbidden his son to go there. Times Square today is a pedestrian plaza filled with flashing neon signs and upscale shops. But in 1960 Times Square was filled with male and female prostitutes, alcoholics, strip clubs, and adult movie theaters. According to biographer Gwenda Blair, Donald was attracted to the many novelty stores in the area that sold knives. Over the course of several months he accumulated a cache of long, dangerous knives, some with blades nearly 12 inches (30 cm) long.

> "[My father assumed] that a little military training might be good for me. I wasn't thrilled about the idea but it turned out he was right."[9]
>
> — Donald Trump

Fred discovered the knife collection and was furious when he learned that Donald had been traveling to Times Square without adult supervision. Combined with his troubles at school, Fred decided Donald needed some radical discipline. When eighth grade began Donald was enrolled in the New York Military Academy, a strict boarding school 75 miles (120 km) north of Queens. As Trump writes in *The Art of the Deal*, "[My

Fred and Mary Trump

Trump's parents, Fred and Mary, did not spoil their children. Each Trump child was assigned a list of chores. They were questioned about their homework, were forbidden to call each other names, and the girls could not wear lipstick. And as *Washington Post* political journalists Michael Kranish and Marc Fisher explain, Trump was strongly influenced by his parents:

> A workaholic, Fred would take Donald with him to construction sites and to his headquarters, a converted dentist's office near Coney Island, where the boy would absorb his father's attention to detail and obsession with cutting costs. . . . Fred would pick unused nails off the floor and return them to his carpenters. He saved money on floor cleanser by ordering lab analyses of store-bought products, buying the ingredients, and having them mixed to produce his own.

> A fastidious, formal man who wore a jacket and tie even at home, Fred could be dour and socially awkward. His wife, Mary, relished attention, thrusting herself to the center of parties and social gatherings. She also loved pomp, sitting for hours to watch the coronation of Queen Elizabeth. A homemaker, Mary devoted herself to charitable work. . . . Mary had various medical problems . . . [and] from his mother, Donald inherited a wariness about catching germs that led to years as an adult when he avoided shaking hands.

Michael Kranish and Marc Fisher, *Trump Revealed: An American Journey of Ambition, Ego, Money, and Power.* New York: Simon & Schuster, 2016, pp. 36–37.

father assumed] that a little military training might be good for me. I wasn't thrilled about the idea but it turned out he was right. . . . I stayed through my senior year, and along the way I learned a lot about discipline, and about channeling my aggression into achievement."[9]

Donald channeled his competitive personality into winning; he won contests for the cleanest room, the best-made bed, and the shiniest shoes. He was awarded numerous medals for neatness and order. Donald's grades improved, and he rose in rank from private to corporal to supply sergeant. In 1963, during his senior year, Donald was

The Trump family home (pictured) in the exclusive Jamaica Estates neighborhood of Queens, New York, boasted twenty-three rooms. Household affairs were carried out by a staff that included a cook, a maid, and a chauffeur.

appointed to the prestigious position of captain of the cadets in which he oversaw a forty-five-man platoon. By this time Donald was 6 feet 2 inches (188 cm) tall and wore an aura of authority with his full dress uniform and white gloves.

Donald graduated in May 1964 but had no intention of pursuing a military career. At the time the Vietnam War was escalating, and thousands of young men were being drafted into the military. Donald decided to go to college, which meant he could avoid the draft as long as he remained in school. He chose to attend Fordham University in the Bronx so he could live at home and commute to school in his red Austin-Healey sports car.

His First Success in Real Estate

Donald's father had often profited from buying properties that were in foreclosure. In this situation, an owner is unable to make mortgage payments on a loan for a home or other piece of property. The bank that made the loan can then seize the property and offer it to another buyer. Foreclosures are often a good bargain since banks usually want to sell the seized property as quickly as possible. Like his father, Donald saw ways to profit from the purchase of foreclosures. As he explains, "In college, while my friends were reading the comics and the sports pages of newspapers, I was reading listings of . . . foreclosures."[10] One of these listings Donald discovered was for a troubled apartment complex in Cincinnati called Swifton Village. The complex, built in 1962, had twelve hundred apartments but eight hundred were vacant, and the owners had gone bankrupt.

In 1964 Donald convinced his father to buy Swifton Village for $6 million, half of what it had cost to build the complex. Donald was put in charge of restoring the property. In *The Art of the Deal*, Trump describes the complex as a total disaster and lays blame for that condition on the renters:

> The tenants who were living in the project when I took over had ripped the place apart. Many of them had come down from the hills of Kentucky. They were very poor and had seven or eight children, almost no possessions, and no experience living in an apartment complex. They crammed into one-room and two-room apartments, and their children just went wild. They would just destroy the apartments and wreak havoc on the property.[11]

Many of the renters were forced out when Trump raised the rent substantially. With most apartments now empty, the Trumps invested around $800,000 in building improvements, including cleaning, painting, and remodeling. Within a year all of the apartments were rented to

Police in riot gear look on as demonstrators in Washington, DC, protest the Vietnam War. Feeling out of place among fellow students who were protesting and living the 1960s lifestyle, Trump transferred to a university that seemed more suited to his interests.

new tenants. The Trumps sold the building for $12 million, doubling their original investment.

With this sale, Donald Trump had taken his first step toward a lengthy and lucrative career in real estate. Getting to that point would require a change of schools, however. Trump did not have much in common with many of his fellow students at Fordham. As at other universities, many students were protesting the Vietnam War, taking drugs, and living the hippie lifestyle. By contrast, Trump carried an expensive leather briefcase and wore a three-piece business suit to class. Feeling like an outsider, Trump decided to transfer to the Wharton School of Finance and Commerce at the University of Pennsylvania in 1966. The Wharton business school was one of the few in the country that offered a degree in real estate studies. At Wharton, Trump was no outsider; his classmates also came from families that had made their fortunes in real estate. Although some of the other students were far wealthier, Trump was not intimidated. He stood out among his classmates as someone with huge dreams. He often bragged that one day he would be the biggest real estate developer Manhattan had ever seen.

The Trump Organization

After college Trump went to work full-time for his father's real estate company, which focused on renting homes and apartments to middle-class residents of Staten Island, Brooklyn, and Queens. In 1971 Donald took control of the company and renamed it the Trump Organization, the name that is still used today.

Soon after Trump took over the family business, it became the focus of a racial discrimination investigation. In 1972 the Urban League, a civil rights group, sent out undercover investigators, called testers, to Trump-owned apartments in Brooklyn. When African American testers tried to rent Trump apartments, they were either refused or steered to other properties where people of color lived. When white Urban League testers tried to rent the same apartments, they were immediately offered leases. When caught in the act of discrimination, apartment managers who oversaw leasing said they were following orders given by the Trumps. Once the Urban League felt it had proof of a pattern of

Trump and the Military Draft

Trump graduated from college in 1968, the year that the US military drafted three hundred thousand men to fight in Vietnam. Although Trump lost his draft deferment upon graduation, he was able to avoid the draft. An army physical disqualified him for medical reasons. Although the military does not specify what the medical condition was, Trump later said it was because he had bone spurs on both heels. Bone spurs are protrusions on the heel that can cause pain when walking long distances. This problem earned Trump the military classification of 1-Y; this meant he was medically disqualified except in cases of national emergency. The classification remained in effect until 1972, when it was changed for unknown reasons to 4-F, not qualified for service. He later said the bone spurs healed and never caused him any more problems.

discrimination, it gave its findings to the US Justice Department's Civil Rights Division.

In October 1973 the Justice Department announced the filing of a racial bias case: *United States of America v. Fred C. Trump, Donald Trump, and Trump Management, Inc.* A Justice Department press release said the Trumps had violated the law "by refusing to rent and negotiate rentals with blacks, requiring different rental terms and conditions because of race, and misrepresenting that apartments were not available."[12]

Trump fought the charges—both in the media and in the courts. The day after the case was filed, Trump told the *New York Times* the charges "are absolutely ridiculous. We never have discriminated, and we never would."[13] Trump's lawyers also responded to the charges by filing a countersuit against the Justice Department that December. In the countersuit Trump sought $100 million in damages, contending that the Justice Department had made false and misleading claims against Trump Management (a subsidiary of the Trump Organization). The countersuit also accused the government of trying to force the Trumps to rent apartments to people on welfare.

> "[Donald Trump] is tall, lean and blond, with dazzling white teeth, and . . . rides around town in a chauffeured silver Cadillac with his initials, DJT, on the plates."[14]
>
> — Judy Klemestrud, *New York Times* reporter

A month after it was filed, Trump's countersuit was dismissed by a judge. The Justice Department continued to pursue its discrimination case against the Trump Organization. In 1975 the Trumps decided to settle with the Justice Department. They admitted no wrongdoing but signed a court order prohibiting them from discriminating against any person in the sale or rental of property in the future.

Building an Image

In the years immediately following the settlement of the discrimination case, Trump sought ways to improve his public image. The *New York Times* gave him one opportunity to do this when, in 1976, it asked

Trump to participate in a personality profile. He was eager to cooperate. The story, headlined "Donald Trump, Real Estate Promoter, Builds Image and He Buys Buildings," ran on November 1 and presented Trump in a very favorable light. In the article, reporter Judy Klemestrud wrote that "he is tall, lean and blond, with dazzling white teeth, and he looks ever so much like [actor] Robert Redford. He rides around town in a chauffeured silver Cadillac with his initials, DJT, on the plates. He dates slinky fashion models, belongs to the most elegant clubs and, at only 30 years of age, estimates that he is worth 'more than $200 million.'"[14]

Anyone who knew Donald Trump during his early years would not have been surprised by Klemestrud's article. Trump fell in love with Manhattan during his teenaged escapades to Times Square and was strongly focused on making real estate deals when most of his peers were protesting and partying. As a third-generation real estate developer, Trump had become everything he dreamed of in high school: a rich and famous jet-setter who was on his way to the top.

Chapter 2

Winning and Losing in Business

Donald Trump was not yet a household name in 1976, but he was clearly joining the ranks of New York's up-and-comers. The Trump Organization had a large number of real estate holdings, and Trump believed that keeping his name in the press was the best way to further boost his fortunes. Toward that end, Trump granted nearly all interview requests from the media. If no journalists were calling, Trump would pick up the phone and call them. He would remind reporters that he was working on projects that would one day be the biggest and best Manhattan had ever seen.

When Trump appeared in public he dressed flamboyantly, favoring burgundy suits and white silk shirts with his initials stitched onto the cuffs. He met with business associates and politicians at the trendiest Manhattan clubs and restaurants to discuss real estate deals, development projects, and politics. One of Trump's favorite clubs was Maxwell's Plum, where he first met twenty-seven-year-old Ivana Zelnicekova.

Trump was immediately attracted to the beautiful and charming Czech fashion model. Soon they were the hottest pair in Manhattan, as reporter Prachi Gupta recalls: "Ivana and Donald Trump were the 'It Couple' in New York City, seen as the very symbol of opulence, glamour, and luxury."[15] After a whirlwind romance, Trump and Zelnicekova were married in 1977. The lavish ceremony was covered like a royal wedding by the press. Soon after the marriage the Trumps started a family: Donald Jr. was born in 1977, daughter Ivanka came along in 1981, and Eric was born in 1984.

First Big Development Project

At the time of his marriage, Trump was working on his first major real estate development project in Manhattan. The Commodore Hotel, located on East Forty-Second Street, was right next to Manhattan's Grand Central Terminal—the busiest train station in the United States. When the thirty-story Commodore was built in 1919 it was considered the height of luxury, but the hotel was a rat-infested ruin by the mid-1970s. Trump saw the Commodore as an opportunity, a building he could remake into a first-class hotel. As he wrote in *The Art of the Deal,* "I could envision a huge home run."[16]

To achieve his goal, Trump put together a deal that included huge government tax breaks over a forty-year period. He also got help with a much-needed construction loan. Because Trump did not yet have a track record as a developer, he could not obtain the loan on his own. For that, he turned to his father and to the Hyatt hotel chain, which had agreed to run the Commodore when the remodel was completed. Hyatt and Fred Trump jointly guaranteed a $70 million loan that committed the two parties to finishing the project if Donald proved unable to do so.

Work on the Commodore (which was to be renamed the Grand Hyatt Hotel) began in May 1978, and the job was bigger than anything Trump had ever attempted. The entire building had to be gutted, and parts of the rusty steel frame were in need of major repairs. Once the structural repairs were completed, the interior would need a full makeover. Ivana Trump had studied business and decorating during her college years, so Trump asked her to help out with that aspect of the remodel. She was named vice president of the project, in charge of overseeing interior design. This was an unusual move at the time, as family friend Nikki Haskell explains: "It was unheard of for a businessman in those circles to give his wife, his *new* wife . . . such great responsibilities. . . . Many rich men don't allow their wives to come to their office."[17]

> "Ivana and Donald Trump were the 'It Couple' in New York City, seen as the very symbol of opulence, glamour, and luxury."[15]
>
> — Prachi Gupta, journalist

The fourteen-hundred-room Grand Hyatt was completed on September 25, 1980. The timing was a lucky break. By the time the hotel opened, revitalization of the entire neighborhood was well under way. Dozens of other hotels, apartment buildings, and offices were under construction in Midtown. This helped make the Grand Hyatt an instant success and elevated Trump's profile to that of a skilled property developer. The project also changed Trump's life, as he wrote in 1987: "If I hadn't . . . gone on to develop the Grand Hyatt, I'd probably be back in Brooklyn today, collecting rents. I had a lot riding on [that first project]."[18]

Fifth Avenue Demolition

As work progressed on the Grand Hyatt, Trump often drove around Manhattan in his limousine looking for his next project. In the late 1970s the Bonwit Teller building on Fifth Avenue became a major focus for Trump. The upscale women's department store was facing financial difficulties and was selling off its properties. In 1979 Trump was able to buy the building for $25 million. And Trump did not need his father to back him on his new venture. With the success of the Grand Hyatt he was able to obtain a $100 million construction loan to build his dream project, the Trump Tower. But first the Bonwit Teller building needed to be demolished.

> "If I hadn't . . . gone on to develop the Grand Hyatt, I'd probably be back in Brooklyn today, collecting rents."[18]
>
> — Donald Trump

The Bonwit Teller building, erected in 1929, was an architectural gem beloved by New Yorkers because of its art deco features. Art deco is a decorative style that was popular in the 1920s and 1930s that emphasized bold geometric designs and angular figures. The façade of the Bonwit Teller building was decorated with two highly stylized seminude female figures carved into 15-foot (5 m) limestone panels. Trump promised to preserve the artwork and present it as a gift to the New York Metropolitan Museum of Art. However, as Trump writes in *The Art of the Deal,* preserving the sculptures turned out to be a bigger and more time-consuming challenge than expected. Trump worried that

Donald and Ivana Trump attend a reception. At Donald's request, Ivana oversaw interior design work for the Grand Hyatt.

the delay would cost him money. Rather than bog down the demolition and construction, he ordered his workers to jackhammer the sculptures off the building. They were destroyed in the process. The following day a photo of the workmen demolishing the sculptures appeared on the front page of the *New York Times,* generating great rancor toward Trump from countless New York art lovers. A short time later the entire building was demolished and the site readied for Trump's grand project.

The Trump Tower Rises

Work began on Trump Tower in 1980 after the Bonwit Teller building was demolished. The 664-foot-high (202 m) Trump Tower was designed by architect Der Scutt (who made his reputation as designer of several of Manhattan's most prominent buildings). The building featured a sawtooth façade stretching from the lower floors to the top of the building. This jagged layout provides stunning views in two directions for most of the luxury condominiums in the fifty-eight-story building. Trump planned to fill the first five floors of his flagship building with trendy shops while the next eleven floors would hold lavish offices, including one for the Trump Organization.

Construction on Trump Tower was hurried; crews began work before full plans were completed. They worked eighteen-hour shifts, six days a week, pouring enough concrete to build two stories a day. As construction on Trump Tower proceeded, Trump continued to make deals. He bought two iconic New York apartment buildings with plans to demolish them. After running into stubborn opposition from the tenants, Trump turned the apartments into luxury condominiums.

A year into the construction of Trump Tower, Trump received some tragic news. On September 26, 1981, his older brother, Fred, died of a heart attack at age forty-three. Fred had entered the family real estate business, but he was mild mannered and never seemed able to please his stern father. As Donald puts it, "Our family environment, the competitiveness, was a negative for Fred. . . . Freddy just wasn't a killer."[19] Fred's early death, blamed on excessive smoking and drinking, would lead Donald to avoid cigarettes and alcohol his entire life.

When Trump Tower opened in 1983, the project was an instant success. The building's 266 condos sold for a combined total of $277 million, an amount that allowed Trump to pay off his entire loan and earn a huge profit. Numerous superstar celebrities purchased condos in the building. Among them were pop star Michael Jackson, film director Steven Spielberg, and talk show host Johnny Carson. Premium retailers such as Mondi (clothing) and Harry Winston (jewelry) paid up to $1 million a year to rent space in the tower.

In March 1984 Donald, Ivana, and their three children moved into a three-story, fifty-three-room penthouse atop Trump Tower. The Trump home featured gold-plated trim, marble and onyx bathrooms, crystal chandeliers, fountains, and 29-foot-high (9 m) ceilings decorated with

murals of cherubs copied from fifteenth-century Renaissance paintings. The gilded Trump palace was featured on a September 1984 episode of *Lifestyles of the Rich and Famous*, a television show about the extravagant lives of entertainers, sports figures, and business moguls. As Trump said to the camera, "I believe in spending maybe more money than other people would think almost rational."[20]

Building a Dream

Trump was now a celebrity businessman and the most famous landlord and real estate developer in America. He fielded dozens of requests from television shows and appeared on the cover of numerous national magazines. When asked the secret of his success, Trump told reporters he liked to think big. And it was this sort of thinking that led him to look beyond Manhattan for his next big project. Trump planned to build a resort hotel and casino in Atlantic City, New Jersey, where voters had legalized gambling in 1976. In *The Art of the Deal*, Trump, who does not gamble, explains his motives: "It's nice to build a successful hotel. It's a lot better to build a hotel attached to a huge casino that can earn fifty times what you'd ever earn renting hotel rooms. You're talking a whole different order of magnitude."[21]

> "I believe in spending maybe more money than other people would think almost rational."[20]
>
> — Donald Trump

In 1982 Trump struck a deal with Harrah's Entertainment, a global casino gaming company. He would build the $250 million hotel and casino called Harrah's at Trump Plaza, and Harrah's Entertainment would run the facility. In 1984 the six-hundred-room hotel, with seven restaurants, an auditorium, and a huge gaming floor, held its grand opening. Unlike Trump's previous projects, the casino was not a major success; it only profited a disappointing $144,000 in the first six months of operation.

With his first casino barely making a profit, Trump surprised business analysts by borrowing $320 million to build another casino across the street from Harrah's. Trump Castle, the new casino, opened in 1985; marketing materials called it the crown jewel of Atlantic City. In 1986 Trump went further into debt, buying out Harrah's share of the first casino, which was renamed Trump Plaza Hotel and Casino.

In the middle of his casino-building boom, Trump produced the book *Trump: The Art of the Deal,* ghostwritten by Tony Schwartz. In the

Courting the Press

In the early 1980s Donald Trump told the *New York Times* that he accomplished more in seven years than others did in a lifetime. Boastful pronouncements like this made Trump a magnet for reporters. Donald and Ivana appeared in a September 1983 article in *Town & Country*, a magazine that caters to the rich and famous. A month later Trump was the subject of a ten-page article in *Gentleman's Quarterly*, which was the top-selling men's magazine of the era. In 1984 Trump appeared on the cover of the *New York Times Sunday Magazine,* which contained a long article about his expanding empire. The media coverage made Trump a star and boosted his appeal among average New Yorkers. As Trump's lawyer, Jerry Schrager, recalls, "I was constantly astonished at how people received him and his projects. I would sit there, sometimes across the table from some pretty sophisticated, intelligent folks, and the majority bought into it. The general public bought into it. The man on the street, the cabdrivers, everybody wanted to touch him and shake his hand."

Quoted in Gwenda Blair, *The Trumps: Three Generations of Builders and a Presidential Candidate.* New York: Simon & Schuster, 2015, p. 311.

book Trump celebrated his talents, abilities, and ambitions while providing advice for aspiring business leaders. He bragged about the huge tax breaks he obtained, derided his critics, and boasted about his successes. Trump told readers that they should emulate him and think big. And in 1988 Trump decided he wanted a bigger piece of Atlantic City.

Trump had his eye on a huge casino called the Taj Mahal that was half finished when its owner died. Trump bought the building for $96 million, but it would cost him $525 million to complete construction before it opened in 1990. Despite the extraordinary costs, the Taj Mahal was attractive to Trump for several reasons: it was the largest casino in the nation and the tallest building in New Jersey. As Trump describes it, "Everything is much bigger than it should be. It's built as a dream."[22]

Falling Fast

Trump's casino dream quickly turned into a nightmare. Since 1982 Trump had borrowed billions of dollars, and his casinos were struggling. When the shiny new Taj Mahal opened, gamblers abandoned Trump's two older casinos. And Trump was not just buying casinos. In 1988 he acquired the Plaza Hotel in Manhattan for nearly $500 million. The following year he bought the Eastern Airlines Shuttle for $380 million and renamed it the Trump Shuttle. Trump envisioned his airline as a luxury service; he spent $1 million remodeling every jet, installing gold-plated bathroom fixtures and mahogany paneling. However, commuters did not want fancy jets for short shuttle flights—they wanted inexpensive and reliable flights. The airline never made a profit.

By the 1990s the Atlantic City casinos were in bad financial shape. Trump was worried that if a few high-stakes gamblers won large bets, his casinos would not be able to afford the payouts. And Trump's worsening financial situation was not a secret. Major newspapers across the country reported that Trump had accumulated $3.4 billion in debt and could not make payments on the loans. In 1991 the Taj Mahal was forced into business bankruptcy. The following year Trump was in bankruptcy court two more times, for the Plaza and the Castle. The bankruptcies were filed under a provision

Donald Trump announces his intention to buy the Eastern Airlines Shuttle, which he renamed Trump Shuttle. His planned luxury airline fell short of making a profit.

Trump: The Art of the Deal

Donald Trump's book, *Trump: The Art of the Deal*, is mostly about his business philosophy. It includes these and other maxims: "Think big." "Maximize your options." "Deliver the goods." It also explains his penchant for sensationalism and controversy. "People may not always think big themselves, but they can still get very excited by those who do. That's why a little hyperbole never hurts. People want to believe that something is the biggest and the greatest and the most spectacular."

But the book reveals more about Trump than his views about business. As Jim Geraghty of the *National Review* writes, it presents a "fascinating time capsule, a long look at a 40-year-old mogul on his way to becoming the country's most famous businessman." It presents readers with a side of the man many people today might not recognize. "The Trump that emerges," Geraghty continues, "is a much softer, warmer, and probably happier figure than the man dominating the airwaves today. He comes across as a garrulous uncle, reverent to his father and mother, still wildly enamored with his wife Ivana, and taking delight in his growing children. He writes about Ivana with fondness, heaping praise on her skill at managing the Trump Castle casino. He chuckles that he never expected to spend parts of his mornings examining kindergarten classrooms at private schools for Ivanka and Eric."

Quoted in Richard Feloni, "Donald Trump's Core Business Philosophy from His Bestselling 1987 Book 'The Art of the Deal'," *Business Insider*, June 16, 2015.

Jim Geraghty, "In *The Art of the Deal*, Trump Shows His Soft Side," *National Review*, September 24, 2015. www.nationalreview.com.

called Chapter 11, which allows troubled companies to stay in business while reorganizing their business practices and reducing debt. A bankruptcy judge removed Trump from his management position, and he was forced to surrender half his stake in the casinos. Trump also had to sell the Trump Shuttle and his $29 million, 282-foot (86 m) yacht, the *Trump Princess.*

Keeping His Personal Wealth Intact

Trump would declare bankruptcy on three more occasions on his hotel and casino holdings before 2010. When his six bankruptcies became an issue in the 2016 presidential debate with Hillary Clinton, Trump stated, "I have used the laws of this country . . . the [bankruptcy] chapter laws, to do a great job for my company, for myself, for my employees, for my family."[23]

Declaring bankruptcy might have benefited Trump and his family, but it had a negative effect on thousands of working-class Americans. Trump owed millions to independent business concerns, including construction contractors, restaurant suppliers, cleaning companies, and others involved in building and maintaining his massive casino empire. Bankruptcy allowed Trump to not pay what he originally owed these small business owners, and many of them were forced to declare bankruptcy themselves. Beth Rosser's family building supply business nearly collapsed along with the Taj Mahal finances. According to Rosser, "Trump crawled his way to the top on the back of little guys.. . . He had no regard for thousands of men and women who worked on those projects."[24]

> "Trump crawled his way to the top on the back of little guys. . . . He had no regard for thousands of men and women who worked on those projects."[24]
>
> — Beth Rosser, businesswoman

Trump spent his life learning about real estate from his father and found early success in a business he knew well. When he ventured into the high-stakes world of casinos, he may have overextended himself. But even as he lost billions of dollars, Trump never declared personal bankruptcy. Trump managed to keep most of his wealth, the Trump Tower, his penthouse, and his ability to make the next big deal.

Chapter 3

Celebrity and Politics

Donald Trump has never been one to shy away from speaking his mind. In 1987 he paid thousands of dollars for a full-page open letter to all Americans that ran in the *New York Times, Washington Post,* and *Boston Globe.* In the letter, Trump argued that America's foreign policy needed some backbone. He questioned US financial support for wealthy nations like Saudi Arabia and Japan. His letter boldly stated, "Tax these wealthy nations, not America. End our huge deficits, reduce our taxes and let America's economy grow unencumbered by the cost of defending those who can easily afford to pay us for the defense of their freedom. Let's not let our great country be laughed at anymore."[25]

Many of those who saw the ads wondered what had inspired the real estate mogul to suddenly jump into the arena of foreign policy debate. One idea was that Trump planned to run as a Republican candidate in the upcoming 1988 presidential election. Another idea was that he was trying to generate publicity for his recently published book, *The Art of the Deal.* Whatever his intention, Trump did not run in 1988. But the ads exhibited one of Trump's well-known personality traits: attracting attention to himself while keeping people guessing about his motives and ambitions.

Trump's political views and business deals were not the only thing that attracted public attention. In 1989 Donald and Ivana Trump were involved in a bitter divorce battle; their marriage ended in 1992. Donald had been involved in an affair with a twenty-five-year-old model named Marla Maples, and the drama played out weekly in tabloid newspapers. Trump and Maples married in November 1993, one

Donald Trump and Marla Maples leave a Florida hospital with their newborn baby girl in 1993. The Trump-Maples wedding attracted prominent politicians, celebrities, and many members of the media.

month after their daughter, Tiffany Ariana Trump, was born. Trump's second wedding was a huge media affair. Ninety photographers and seventeen international television crews covered the event, which was attended by a who's who of politicians, celebrities, and star athletes.

The Business of Beauty

Marriage never stopped Trump from cultivating an image as a ladies' man. He was always appearing in photographs with models, actresses, and beauty queens. As Trump biographers Michael Kranish and Marc Fisher explain, "Trump sold his products—casinos, hotels, condos—in part by surrounding himself with symbols of the high life, most especially beautiful women. . . . At his public appearances, Trump would have seemed naked without gorgeous women by his side."[26]

Many of the beautiful women who accompanied Trump were involved with one of his first ventures in the entertainment business. In 1996 Trump purchased the Miss Universe pageants, which included the Miss USA and Miss Teen USA competitions. The women in Trump's life soon got involved in the pageant business. Maples hosted the Miss Universe and Miss USA pageants in 1996 and 1997; fifteen-year-old Ivanka hosted the Miss Teen USA pageant in 1997. That same year Trump appointed a woman as the first female president of the Miss Universe organization. Trump took pride in the pageants. He often stated his belief that they helped empower hundreds of participants with career opportunities they would not have had otherwise.

These comments differed sharply—in tone and substance—from other comments Trump made about women around the same period. In more than twenty appearances on the nationally broadcast Howard Stern radio show between the late 1990s and mid-2000s, Trump took part in what many people consider to be crass and insulting conversations with the show's host. In a 2005 appearance, for instance, Stern asked Trump how he would rate actress Nicollette Sheridan on a scale of 1 to 10. Trump responded: "A person who is very flat chested is very hard to be a ten."[27] That same year, again on Stern's show, Trump told about his frequent visits to the beauty pageant dressing rooms when the contestants were changing outfits: "I'll go backstage before a show, and everyone's getting dressed and ready and everything else. . . . And I'm allowed to go in because I'm the owner of the pageant. . . . You know, they're standing there with no clothes. And

> "Trump sold his products—casinos, hotels, condos—in part by surrounding himself with symbols of the high life, most especially beautiful women."[26]
>
> — Michael Kranish and Marc Fisher, Trump biographers

Donald Trump appears onstage at the 2013 Miss USA Pageant. Beside him are Miss Universe 2012 Olivia Culpo (left) and pageant hosts Nick Jonas and Giuliana Rancic (right). Trump owned the pageants and took pride in them.

you see these incredible-looking women. And so I sort of get away with things like that."[28]

Those who took an interest in Trump's activities were left to wonder which of the various public personas reflected the real Donald Trump. Those who worked with Trump say that his swagger was an act meant to boost his profile and add gloss to his brand. As his attorney, Jay Goldberg, states, Trump was more of a chocolate-loving homebody than a swinger: "I only remember him finishing the day [by] going home, not necessarily with a woman but with a bag of candy. . . . He planned his next project, read the blueprints, met with the lawyers, never raising his voice, never showing off, never nasty to anybody in the office, a gentleman."[29]

A Natural Showman

One thing that most anyone who watched Trump could agree on was that he was a natural showman—and he particularly excelled at self-promotion. These qualities did not go unnoticed in the world of television and movie entertainment. Throughout the 1990s and early 2000s Trump made short appearances, called cameos, on America's most popular television shows, including *The Fresh Prince of Bel-Air, The Nanny, Spin City,* and *Sex and the City.* Trump also played himself in blockbuster films, including *Home Alone 2: Lost in New York* (1992) and *Zoolander* (2001). Trump developed a reputation among directors as a natural: he remembered his lines, did not appear nervous in front of a camera, and required little in the way of coaching.

Maples appeared with Trump in several of those cameos—exuding an image of a happy couple. But that image soon collapsed when the two divorced in 1999. Shortly after that time Trump began dating another fashion model. Twenty-nine-year-old Melania Knauss was born in Slovenia and began her modeling career at age sixteen. After moving to the United States in 1996, Melania's career was managed by Trump Model Management, an agency owned by Trump. Knauss and Trump married in 2005. The reception at Trump's Mar-a-Lago estate in Palm Beach, Florida, was attended by a glittering array of celebrities, including P. Diddy, Shaquille O'Neal, and even Bill and Hillary Clinton. Melania gave birth to their son, Barron, in 2006—the same year Melania became a US citizen.

> "[Trump] planned his next project, read the blueprints, met with the lawyers, never raising his voice, never showing off, never nasty to anybody in the office, a gentleman."[29]
>
> — Jay Goldberg, attorney

The Apprentice

Television producer Mark Burnett was among those who had recognized Trump's uncanny ability to attract massive media attention—and Trump came to mind when Burnett began thinking about a new show.

Trump Considers Running for President

In 1999 Trump appeared on the television talk show *Larry King Live* to announce that he was leaving the Republican Party to join the Reform Party. Trump's new party had about ten thousand members until 1998, when professional wrestler Jesse "the Body" Ventura was elected governor of Minnesota on the Reform Party ticket. Trump, a long-time fan of the World Wrestling Federation, was fascinated by Ventura's surprising political victory. In January 2000 Trump flew to Minnesota to find out how Ventura managed to get elected despite starting out with little support from the public or the media. Ventura advised Trump to use the Internet to solicit donations and spread his message. After the meeting Trump realized he could use a presidential run to raise money while boosting his business interests. As Trump told journalist Jerry Useem in April 2000, "It's very possible that I could be the first presidential candidate to run and make money on it."

By April 2000 Trump was seriously considering running for president as a Reform Party candidate. A Gallup poll had shown that Trump was a known figure to 98 percent of Americans. This made his dreams of moving into the White House seem attainable. However, by the summer of 2000 Trump had decided not to run for president. He did not think it was possible for him to win without the backing of the Republican Party, which was moving to elect George W. Bush.

Quoted in Jerry Useem, "What Does Donald Trump Really Want?," *Fortune*, April 3, 2000. http://fortune.com.

Burnett was the creator of the reality show *Survivor*. Millions of viewers tuned in every week to watch contestants as they battled to survive on isolated tropical islands or in the Australian outback. One afternoon in 2003, while shooting an episode of *Survivor*, Burnett came up with an idea for a new show. The idea came to him, he later said, when he looked down and saw what appeared to be two colonies of ants fighting to the death. This gave Burnett the idea to create a *Survivor*-type show in an urban setting. It would depict aggressive job seekers battling each other in New York's concrete jungle.

Burnett needed a tough, colorful host who could attract an audience. Trump seemed like a natural. Burnett and Trump met at Trump Tower, and after a one-hour meeting they shook hands and agreed to produce a show called *The Apprentice*. The show would feature sixteen job seekers competing for a position at one of Trump's companies.

Contestants would sell products, raise money for charities, create advertising campaigns, and perform other business-related tasks. Each week Trump would fire one of the contestants who failed to please him.

The Apprentice premiered in January 2004 and was an immediate hit. Within weeks Trump was known for the catchphrase he uttered at the end of every show: "You're fired!" This led Trump to trademark the catchphrase so no one else could use it on a television show or in a movie without paying royalties. The success of the show resulted in numerous spin-offs, including *The Celebrity Apprentice*, which featured well-known people as contestants.

From his first meeting with Burnett, Trump recognized the value of *The Apprentice* as a way to promote the Trump brand. Episodes would feature his luxurious jet, the Trump Tower, the Taj Mahal casino, and his Mar-a-Lago estate. After the show's ratings jumped into the top ten in 2005, Trump took full advantage of its success. He introduced a host of new Trump-brand products, including neckties, bottled water, lamps, cologne, a credit card, and even frozen steaks. He also created Trump University, a series of courses designed to teach ordinary people how to get rich buying and selling real estate.

In addition to increasing Trump's wealth, *The Apprentice* did something else: the show helped humanize Trump by portraying him as someone more complicated than the model-loving, power-hungry tycoon featured in the tabloids. As Trump explained to talk show host Larry King in 2004, the show helped people realize "I'm highly educated, which until *The Apprentice* most people didn't know. They thought I was a barbarian. . . . [But] I do have great feelings for people."[30]

> "I'm highly educated, which until *The Apprentice* most people didn't know. They thought I was a barbarian. . . . [But] I do have great feelings for people."[30]
>
> —Donald Trump

The success of *The Apprentice* enhanced Trump's celebrity status. He could no longer walk down the street in New York without being mobbed by adoring fans. This new level of attention inspired Trump to consider getting into politics. On more than one occasion he told

Burnett that people loved him so much he could run for president—and win.

This was not the first time Trump had expressed presidential ambitions. In 1999 he had joined the Reform Party and had considered running for president on the Reform ticket. However, the Reform Party was a minor political movement. With Democrats and Republicans dominating the political scene, third-party candidates like those in the Reform Party could not compete successfully. With this in mind, Trump decided not to run for president in 2000.

Leading the Birther Movement

Trump left the Reform Party in 2001 and registered as a Democrat. In the following years he confounded political observers by changing his party affiliation several times. He voted as a Republican in 2003 and as a Democrat again in 2005. Trump also gave money to both political parties over the years; between 1989 and 2010 he gave a total of $175,860 in political donations to both Democrats and Republicans. In 2015, when asked by conservative radio host Howie Carr about his party loyalty, Trump responded: "If you're gonna be a business person, even in the United States, you wanna get along with all sides because you're gonna need things from everybody. And you wanna get along with all sides, it's very important."[31]

In the 2008 presidential race, Trump voted for the Republican candidate John McCain. But in a 2009 interview with Larry King, Trump heaped praise on the winning candidate, Barack Obama: "Well I really like him. . . . I think that he's really doing a nice job in terms of representation of this country. . . . I think he's doing a really good job."[32]

By the time Obama was preparing to run for a second term, however, Trump's views on the president had undergone a drastic change. Trump began promoting the idea, which had surfaced in the months before Obama's 2008 election victory, that the president was born in Kenya, Africa, and therefore was not eligible to run for president. This

Trump's Views About Family

Although Donald Trump is twice divorced, he has frequently talked about his close relationships with his children. Maggie Gallagher of the conservative *National Review* describes herself as "no fan of Trump's" but praises his family values. "Trump did a lot of things right as a divorced dad," she writes. "All his older children report feeling he was always available to them if they needed him. He didn't spend a lot of time with his young kids, but he succeeded in letting them know that they mattered to him. And most important of all, he fostered their bonds with their mothers."

Trump has five children. He has two sons and a daughter with his first wife Ivana, one daughter with his second wife Marla, and one son with his current wife Melania. The four oldest of his children all spoke on behalf of their father at the 2016 Republican National Convention.

At various times Trump has talked about the importance of family. He has spoken publicly about his love and appreciation for his older brother Fred Trump Jr., who died in 1981. And in a 2016 conversation with Wisconsin college students, he offered this definition of success: "To me, a successful person has a great family who loves the family, loves the children and the children love him or her. To me, that's a much more successful person than a person that's made a million dollars or 10 million dollars."

Maggie Gallagher, "Trump's Family Values," *National Review*, April 16, 2016.

accusation, which had mainly circulated on conspiracy websites and right-wing talk shows, had already been disproved. Obama was born in Hawaii. His mother, Ann Dunham, was born in Kansas, and his father, Barack Obama Sr., was from Kenya. In 2008 Obama had even released a copy of his birth certificate, which clearly stated that he was born on August 4, 1961, at 7:24 p.m. in Honolulu, Hawaii. Despite such proof of Obama's US birth, Trump used Twitter and media appearances to reignite the birther movement's allegation concerning the president's birth.

In March 2011 a photo of Obama's birth certificate was posted on the Internet for all to see. Trump asserted that the birth certificate was a forgery. His assertion proved false. After examining a physical copy of the birth certificate, the nonpartisan website FactCheck.org wrote,

"[Our] staffers have now seen, touched, examined and photographed the original birth certificate. . . . Our conclusion: Obama was born in the U.S.A. just as he has always said."[33]

Trump refused to back down. In television appearances, he used a communication style that had served him well in the past. When appearing on television, Trump would say he received some information from an unnamed source. He would shake his head and say that he hoped it was not true, but then he would leave listeners in doubt. For example, in April 2011, Trump told *The Today Show,*

I have people that have been studying [Obama's birth certificate] and they cannot believe what they're finding. . . . I would like to have [Obama] show his birth certificate, and can I be honest with you, I hope he can. Because if he can't, if he can't, if he wasn't born in this country, which is a real possibility . . . then he has pulled one of the great cons in the history of politics.[34]

Trump poses with his third wife, Melania (on his immediate left), and their son (front) as well as with his other children and their families in June 2015 after announcing that he is seeking the Republican nomination for president.

Trump's strategy worked. Several polls taken in late 2011 showed that one in five Americans believed that Obama was born outside the United States and therefore was in violation of the law by occupying the office of president.

"It Made Me More Popular"

Trump continued the crusade against Obama. In April 2011 he claimed that he had sent investigators to Hawaii to locate Obama's birth certificate and that they had not been able to find it. He also repeated the discredited claim that Obama's grandmother had witnessed his birth in Kenya. Once again, Obama sought to eliminate any doubt about his birth. In May 2011 he released a longer, more detailed copy of his birth certificate on live television. This was an official state record that is not usually provided to parents after a child is born. This so-called long-form birth certificate still did not satisfy Trump. A year after Obama released the document, Trump once again turned to his favored method of communication. He tweeted, "Was it a birth certificate? You tell me. Some people say that was not his birth certificate. Maybe it was, maybe it wasn't. I'm saying I don't know. Nobody knows."[35]

Trump continued to stoke birther beliefs long past the time when the claims had been discredited by journalists, public officials, and even many conservatives. The birther campaign was seen as an attack on the legitimacy of America's first African American president. As a 2011 editorial in the *New York Times* stated, "It is inconceivable that [Trump's] campaign to portray Mr. Obama as the insidious 'other' would have been conducted against a white president. We doubt that the questions about Mr. Obama's birthplace would have taken off if his father had been from Canada rather than Kenya."[36]

> "Some people say that was not [Obama's] birth certificate. Maybe it was, maybe it wasn't. I'm saying I don't know. Nobody knows."[35]
>
> — Donald Trump

During the 2012 presidential election campaign Donald Trump worked tirelessly on behalf of Republican Mitt Romney. Trump recorded automated phone calls in support of Romney and continually attacked Obama in the media. When Romney lost in November, Trump expressed his frustration in a series of now familiar-sounding blasts on Twitter: "This election is a total sham and travesty." "Let's fight like hell and stop this great and disgusting injustice! The whole world is laughing at us."[37]

Some observers say Trump did not really believe Obama was born in Kenya; he only promoted birtherism to attract a political following. Trump reinforced this theory in 2013 when asked about his birther tweets: "I don't think I went overboard. Actually, I think it made me more popular."[38] Throughout his career, Trump has often sought the limelight. His efforts to get people's attention have at times seemed to reflect the old saying that no publicity is bad publicity. Whether it was his appearance on a television show or racially tinged tweets about the president, Donald Trump ensured people were talking about him, and his brand, nearly every day.

Chapter 4

An Unconventional Candidate

Every four years major political parties in the United States select candidates to run for president through a series of primaries and caucuses held in each state. Republicans and Democrats have different rules, but the winner of each party's contests is usually nominated to run as the party's candidate for president.

The campaigns have long been rough-and-tumble affairs where candidates argue over who is most qualified to run the country. But few of these campaign seasons have been as raucous as the one held by Republicans in 2016. The long election process began in the summer of 2015 when seventeen Republicans declared their intention to seek their party's nomination for president. A series of twelve televised debates followed, each candidate held dozens of campaign events, and the primary elections and caucuses took place between February and June 2016.

Seventeen was a record number of candidates competing for the Republican nomination. Most of them had held public office either at the state or federal level. Their previous experience gave them an understanding of the workings of election campaigns, candidate debates, and the hunt for endorsements. For the most part, they gave carefully crafted speeches meant to appeal to the widest number of voters while trying not to offend anyone.

And then there was Donald Trump, a candidate unlike any of the others—in terms of both experience and temperament. Trump had never held public office, but he understood competition better than most, thanks to his years as a high-stakes real estate developer and as the host and executive producer of the hugely popular reality show *The Apprentice*. Trump understood how successful contestants on reality television shows generated widespread interest on social media. Popular reality

> "We have losers. We have people that don't have it. We have people that are morally corrupt. We have people that are selling this country down the drain."[41]
>
> — Donald Trump

show participants were unpredictable, egotistical, and supremely confident in their beliefs. They insulted and offended people and never apologized. Winning was the only goal, and successful contestants said and did whatever was necessary to mercilessly destroy their opponents. According to media studies professor June Deery, Trump's strategy for victory was based on approaching the political process as a reality show: "Trump's learned that to get attention—which is everything in politics—it's best to be the most outrageous person in the room. . . . [In reality television] extroverted pushy personalities come to the fore."[39]

An Unusual Start to an Unusual Campaign

The reality television tone was set when Trump declared his intention to run for president. Within moments of taking the podium in Trump Tower on June 16, 2015, Trump put aside his notes and said what was on his mind. In the first minute of his presidential declaration—which was covered by print, Internet, and broadcast media—Trump noted that the other Republican hopefuls had "sweated like dogs"[40] when declaring their candidacies. Without mentioning the names of those who had already declared—Jeb Bush, Marco Rubio, and Rand Paul—Trump said they could not be trusted to fight terrorists if they did not even understand the need to turn up their air conditioners. No political campaign had ever been launched with an observation of this sort.

Trump went on to state the themes that he would repeat many times during the campaign: "Our enemies are getting stronger and stronger by the way, and we as a country are getting weaker. . . . We have losers. We have people that don't have it. We have people that are morally corrupt. We have people that are selling this country down the drain." Trump promised to build a wall along the US-Mexico border to halt illegal immigration. "I would build a great wall," Trump said, "and nobody builds walls better than me, believe me, and I'll build them very inexpensively, I will build a great, great wall on our southern border. And I will have Mexico pay for that wall."[41]

Undocumented immigrants climb over the fence that separates the United States and Mexico near Tijuana. Throughout the presidential campaign, Trump promised to build a wall along the length of the US-Mexico border.

A Candidate People Love to Hate

As host of *The Apprentice*, Donald Trump understood that people who become famous on reality television shows like *Keeping Up with the Kardashians* and *Real Housewives* are those whom viewers "love to hate." Erin Martin, who writes for a reality television website, explains how Trump used this concept to dominate the news cycle for eighteen months:

> Hate, in the world of reality TV stars, is a precious and coveted commodity. In fact, if you're a reality star who finds that people don't hate you (at least sometimes), you just might be in trouble. . . . This "love to hate" concept is an important distinction from plain old "dislike," given that [contestants] who are thought of as sniveling, grouchy, [or] boring become universally ignored. . . . If reality stars are going to make it big, they've got to amp up the drama—and by drama, I mean totally insane behavior. Thus, Donald Trump is the perfect Real Housewife—the perfect villain—in the sense that some of us cannot stop talking about [him]. . . . In short, we cannot look away. . . . It is as though Trump has taken the basic tenets of reality TV and shot them up with steroids.

Erin Martin, "Why Donald Trump Is the Perfect 'Real Housewife,'" CNN, October 2, 2016. www.cnn.com.

Millions of people who saw Trump's presidential declaration dismissed his bid as a vanity project, a temporary caper meant to draw attention to his brand. People laughed at Trump's often disjointed delivery and exaggerations. Detractors called him a clown and a carnival barker, and others criticized his racially tinged comments about minorities and immigrants. But many listeners dismissed Trump's most outrageous comments and believed him when he said, "I will be the greatest jobs president that God ever created. I'll bring back our jobs from China, from Mexico, from Japan, from so many places. I'll bring back our jobs, and I'll bring back our money."[42]

Facing Down the Opposition

Whatever people thought of Trump, no one could deny he knew how to draw interest in certain regions of the country, especially the Midwest—often referred to as America's heartland. Trump began his campaign with a series of political rallies that attracted thousands of screaming fans. And Trump played to the adoring crowds; he refused to read from a prepared text and filled his speeches with improvised remarks, egotistical boasts, and a wide assortment of insults. He called foreign policy experts stupid, American generals incompetent, and political leaders of both parties corrupt. He said the American dream was dead and only he knew how to revive it.

With every speech and every tweet, Trump gave his competitors and detractors a seemingly endless source of ammunition. Pundits and candidates from all parts of the political spectrum talked or wrote about Trump's many perceived shortcomings. Two recurring themes were his frequent racist and sexist comments and his absolute lack of foreign policy experience. In a September 2015 interview with conservative radio host Hugh Hewitt, Trump demonstrated his lack of knowledge on foreign affairs when he could not name any of the prominent terrorist groups sowing chaos in Iraq.

Trump's lack of government service was another oft-raised subject. Nearly every candidate in the crowded Republican field had served in some capacity as an elected official. Ted Cruz, Rand Paul, Lindsey Graham, and Marco Rubio were sitting US senators. Chris Christie, Scott Walker, and John Kasich were governors, and Jeb Bush, Mike Huckabee, and Rick Perry were former governors. Only businesswoman Carly Fiorina, neurosurgeon Ben Carson, and Trump had never held elective office.

Many members of the Republican establishment—including prominent elected officials, members of the military and intelligence communities, and even some business leaders—opposed Trump's candidacy. They believed his company's bankruptcies indicated lack of judgment on financial and economic matters. Some even publicly questioned whether he was, in fact, a liberal Democrat because of his previous statements in support of gay rights, gun control, and abortion.

Trump defied the opposition by tapping into a growing and deep-seated distrust of politicians—and frustration with changes in the United States and the world. In public appearances, he spoke with confidence and authority; for the most part, he gave simple answers to complex questions and offered little in the way of details on his plans or policies. Often it seemed that he used language intended to incite emotional reactions—both from his supporters and his critics. And that is what he got: supporters cheered his coarsest comments; critics denounced them. As Michael Kranish and Marc Fisher explain,

> [Trump] may have been a novice politician, but he possessed unerring instincts about what was angering so many Americans. His communication skills were ideally suited to the age of round-the-clock cable, the instantaneous reach of Twitter, and the coarseness of the digital media's raucous, often anonymous conversation. He made provocative, often inaccurate comments that no ordinary candidate would dare utter. . . . He mostly got away with it. Along the way, he rendered many of the older, accepted tactics of politics impotent or obsolete.[43]

Upending the Rules

The first Republican primary debate was hosted by Fox News in August 2015. By this time Trump was leading in the polls, but his political skills remained untested. Trump had never been challenged by seasoned politicians who were skilled in the art of debate. And Trump did seem to falter. He was forced to defend his casino bankruptcies, false statements, and lack of experience in international affairs. Other candidates easily handled questions about their political beliefs and policy positions. But the debate was not remembered for the serious statements made by the others. Instead, when the media dissected the debate the next day, the focus seemed to be on the uncomfortable interchange between Trump and debate moderator Megyn Kelly.

> "[Trump] may have been a novice politician, but he possessed unerring instincts about what was angering so many Americans."[43]
>
> — Michael Kranish and Marc Fisher, Trump biographers

Moderators for the Fox News Republican candidate debates in August 2015 and January 2016 were (from left) Chris Wallace, Megyn Kelly, and Bret Baier. During the first of those two debates Kelly and Trump had an uncomfortable exchange of words.

At one point in the debate, Kelly recited a number of insults and derogatory comments Trump had made about women over the years. Trump turned this perceived weakness into a crowd-pleasing applause line with his response: "I think the big problem this country has—is being politically correct. And I don't frankly have time for total political correctness. And . . . this country doesn't have time either."[44] The next day, rather than letting the matter drop, Trump went on the offensive against Kelly. He called in to the television show *Fox & Friends*, on which he continued to make derogatory comments about Kelly— comments that dominated the news cycle for several days. While the no-holds-barred response might have alienated some, Trump's approval rating actually rose among prospective Republican voters.

The Fox debate had attracted an audience of 24 million, more than any other primary debate in television history, and more than any other live nonsports event. Other news networks quickly saw Trump as a way to attract millions of viewers, boost their ratings, and earn more money from advertisers. Trump became a staple of round-the-clock news coverage.

Trump used the free media attention to his benefit. Instead of running expensive campaign ads like other candidates, he made outrageous statements on Twitter and in public appearances. This allowed him to dominate the twenty-four-hour news cycle as he refused to back down when challenged by critics. By dominating the news, Trump was provided with air time that would have cost an estimated $3 billion to purchase, according to the statistical firm MediaQuest.

> "Covering a Trump event is like watching a 1970s [punk rock] concert from inside a shark cage."[45]
>
> — Seth Stevenson, journalist

Ironically, even as Trump was provided a free platform for his candidacy, he relentlessly criticized the news media. At rallies Trump called reporters disgusting, dishonest scum and encouraged supporters to loudly boo the journalists who were covering his events. Reporters at Trump rallies were corralled into a rectangular press pen made of bike racks. Some were verbally abused, spit on, and thrown to the ground. Seth Stevenson, who covered numerous campaign rallies, described Trump events: "Jeb Bush rallies were not like this. Covering a Jeb event meant freely mingling with 40 people sitting calmly on folding chairs. Covering a Trump event is like watching a 1970s [punk rock] concert from inside a shark cage."[45]

Insulting the Opposition

Although most politicians rely on opposition researchers to dig up negative information about other candidates, Trump did not need anyone to perform that task. During the televised debates, which continued into May 2016, Trump belittled his opponents with catchy nicknames that quickly came to define them in the public mind. When Cruz used the campaign slogan "TRUSTED," Trump turned it around by calling his opponent "Lyin' Ted." Although a senator, Rubio was seen as young and inexperienced—and at 5 feet 10 inches (178 cm), he was shorter than most of the other candidates. Trump labeled him "Little Marco" during a March debate, and the name stuck. Bush, who was initially seen as the

Republican front-runner, failed to generate great excitement. Trump used this against him and repeatedly called Bush "Low Energy Jeb."

Trump went beyond nicknames when it came to throwing his opponents off balance; he taunted, mocked, and insulted them at every chance. Trump said Perry did not need glasses—that he only wore them to seem smart. He commented on Fiorina's looks, saying she was not attractive enough to win. He reserved a special insult for Bush, whose wife is a native of Colombia. Bush had developed a well-researched policy on immigration reform. Trump responded that Bush was forced to "like the Mexican illegals because of his wife."[46]

With Trump hurling insults from center stage during the debates, political journalist Tom Krattenmaker wrote, "[This is] reality TV—the kind that 'entertains' through melodrama highlighting human foolishness and misbehavior at its worst."[47] The networks added to this trend, running commercials for upcoming debates that hyped the contests as if they were wrestling cage matches.

On several occasions Cruz and Rubio tried to throw insults back at Trump, but they mostly fell flat. Bush refused to play by the new

The Twitter President

Trump grew up in an era when television, newspapers, and magazines dominated the media landscape. But throughout his campaign, first for the Republican nomination and then for the presidency, Trump's favored communication tool was Twitter. He considered Twitter a direct line to the American people, unfiltered by reporters and political analysts. By April 2016 Trump had around 7.5 million Twitter followers. That number had grown to nearly 20 million by January 2017. Never before in American history has a presidential candidate used Twitter to communicate his thoughts to the public on such a massive scale. In light of this new development in campaigning, the *New York Times* decided to inventory Trump's Twitter language. In an April 2016 piece the *Times* noted that Trump tweeted insults about more than two hundred people, places, and things between June 2015 and March 2016. His most frequently used words of insult were these: *failing* (on 66 occasions), *lightweight* (37 times), *dumb* or *dummy* (33), *bad!* and *sad!* (31 each), *dopey* (29), *weak* (27), *liar* (27), *loser* (25), *the worst* (22), *boring* (21) *a disaster* (13), *a clown* (11), *stupid* (7), and *not nice* (5).

Trump rules. He campaigned in the traditional manner, spending tens of millions of dollars to run commercials that focused on his policies and achievements as Florida's governor. But as the campaign season moved into 2016, Bush had become irrelevant; he dropped out of the race in February after spending more than $138 million on his quest. (Trump spent around $76 million during the entire primary process, and Cruz spent more than $111 million.)

Trump Wins the Nomination

By the time the primary elections began in February, Trump was in first place among Republicans in all major national polls. Cruz won the first contest in Iowa by a narrow margin. But Trump trounced Cruz by nearly 25 percentage points in the New Hampshire and Nevada contests that followed. Eleven states held elections on March 1, known as Super Tuesday because of its importance. Trump won seven states on Super Tuesday. Cruz won three states. Rubio won one state. Trump was able to rack up most of his wins due to the large field of candidates. While he only averaged around 35 percent of the votes in each state, the remaining votes were split between Cruz, Rubio, Kasich, and Carson. This gave Trump more votes than each of his challengers.

> "I could stand in the middle of 5th Avenue and shoot somebody and I wouldn't lose voters."[48]
>
> — Donald Trump

Throughout the remaining months of the primaries and caucuses, Trump's campaign appearances took on the aura of a rock star meeting adoring fans rather than a candidate seeking the nomination for president. The day before a state contest he would swoop into several cities in his private jet and hold rowdy rallies filled with jeering, cheering, and boos. Although Trump filled his speeches with insults, vague promises, and questionable facts, his supporters remained fiercely loyal. As early as January, at a campaign stop in Iowa, Trump boasted about this devotion. He said, "I could stand in the middle of 5th Avenue and shoot somebody and I wouldn't lose voters."[48]

Political rallies also became the scene of hostile, and sometimes violent, exchanges between Trump supporters and opponents. Protesters on both sides were subjected to verbal and physical attacks. On one occasion, the candidate himself made statements that many saw as inciting violence. These comments were made at a February rally in Nevada, when an anti-Trump activist interrupted Trump's speech. Trump responded: "I love the old days. You know what they used to do to guys like that when they were in a place like this? They'd be carried out on a stretcher, folks. It's true. . . . I'd like to punch him in the face."[49] Several months later, in September, an anti-Trump protester in North Carolina was grabbed by the neck and punched in the face by a supporter.

Despite the turbulent atmosphere surrounding the contest, Trump continued to rack up primary wins while his challengers dropped out of the race one by one. On May 26, 2016, Trump won the Republican nomination for president with14 million votes. Cruz came in second with around 7.8 million votes.

Judging the Public Mood

On July 15, Trump picked Indiana governor Mike Pence as his vice presidential running mate. The selection of Pence was an attempt to win support from mainstream Republicans, who were unhappy with Trump's unexpected triumph. Pence had served in the US House of Representatives from 2001 to 2013 before being elected as governor of Indiana. He was also known as a religious conservative but his strong ties to the Republican base and his reputation as a steady voice for conservatism won over many mainstream Republicans.

Trump and Pence were on a path to victory, although at this point in time few Americans of either political party saw this as the likely outcome. Pundits, pollsters, and many average citizens had underestimated the angry mood of Trump's supporters. Many lived in decaying industrial cities and rural counties where factories, mills, and mines had once provided good jobs. During the great recession of 2008, many had lost their homes and jobs. These people felt they had been left behind culturally and economically in the twenty-first century. Journalist David Wong, who grew up in rural Illinois, explains: "The recession

After winning the Republican nomination, Trump named Indiana governor Mike Pence (pictured) as his vice-presidential running mate. The choice of Pence was aimed at winning support from mainstream Republicans who did not favor Trump.

pounded rural communities, but all the recovery went to the cities. The rate of new businesses opening in rural areas has utterly collapsed. . . . If you don't live in one of these small towns, you can't understand the hopelessness."[50]

Trump voters blamed their woes on a long list of establishment figures, including politicians, the media, bankers, industrialists, and intellectuals who either ignored them, mocked them, or moved their jobs out of the country. Although Trump might have run his campaign like a reality show, he instinctively understood the reality of his supporters. By expertly stoking their anger, Trump saw a path to presidential victory that none of the experts could imagine.

Chapter 5

Trump Wins

Donald Trump's attacks on his Republican challengers had been unrelenting, but he saved his most unsavory remarks for his Democratic challenger, Hillary Clinton. On campaign stops Trump routinely referred to Clinton as "Crooked Hillary." He accused her of corruption and treason. He blamed her for the death and destruction occurring in Libya and Syria and for job losses in the US manufacturing sector. And, on October 9, 2016, during the second of three presidential debates, Trump referred to Clinton as "the devil" and threatened, "If I win I am going to instruct my attorney general to get a special prosecutor to look into your situation—there has never been so many lies and so much deception."[51]

Polar Opposites

Polls throughout most of the campaign indicated that Clinton was ahead of Trump. Some political commentators believed that comments like that were an attempt by Trump to whip up new support among undecided voters—especially those who did not particularly like Clinton. In fact, neither candidate was especially popular with mainstream voters. In June 2016, according to polls, Clinton was viewed unfavorably by 37 percent of Americans, and Trump's unfavorability rating was 53 percent. This made Clinton and Trump the two most unpopular presidential candidates in more than thirty years.

Aside from sharing low approval ratings, Trump and Clinton shared little else. They were polar opposites—in temperament, tone, and political experience. As a former First Lady who later served as a US senator and US secretary of state, Clinton had broad experience in government. Those who supported Clinton described her as someone who relished the technical aspects of lawmaking and governing. Clinton's attention to policy could be seen on her campaign website, which contained detailed positions on the economy, international affairs, renewable energy, and even animal welfare. While Clinton might have had a firm grasp of the issues, her campaign speeches were often criticized as boring and technical. As political analyst Ezra Klein explains, "[Clinton] is careful, calculated, cautious. Her speeches can sound like executive summaries from a committee report, the product of too many authors, too many voices, and too much fear of offense."[52]

> "If I win I am going to instruct my attorney general to get a special prosecutor to look into your situation—there has never been so many lies and so much deception."[51]
>
> — Donald Trump

The lack of excitement for Clinton's candidacy—and the growing enthusiasm for Trump—could be seen at their campaign rallies. While Clinton typically gave speeches to three hundred or four hundred people at community centers and small colleges, Trump was filling arenas, convention centers, and airport hangers with thousands of cheering supporters. And Trump never played it safe, as he demonstrated when he was officially nominated for president at the Republican National Convention in Cleveland, Ohio, in July 2016.

Many Claims, Lots of Blame

When Trump gave his acceptance speech in Cleveland on July 21 he painted a dark and disturbing picture of the United States. Voicing the beliefs of many of his supporters, Trump said Americans had endured a domestic disaster under Obama. He claimed that tens of thousands of illegal immigrants were roaming the streets and threatening peaceful citizens. Trump said crime rates were at a forty-five-year high, despite FBI statistics to the contrary.

In his speech, Trump blamed Clinton for numerous world problems, including the war in Syria, the rise of the terrorist group ISIS, and the attack on the American consulate in Benghazi, Libya:

> After four years of Hillary Clinton [as secretary of state], what do we have? ISIS has spread across the region, and the world. Libya is in ruins, and our Ambassador and his staff were left helpless to die at the hands of savage killers. . . . Syria is engulfed in a civil war and a refugee crisis that now threatens the West. . . . This is the legacy of Hillary Clinton: death, destruction and weakness.[53]

A Voice for the Voiceless

During his seventy-six-minute speech, Trump reiterated the economic message that was so popular among his grassroots supporters. Trump blamed Clinton for supporting tax, trade, and immigration policies that, he contended, had caused the loss of millions of manufacturing jobs. He outlined a plan that he said would improve the quality of life for all Americans:

> I am going to bring our jobs back to Ohio and to America—and I am not going to let companies move to other countries, firing their employees along the way, without consequences. . . . I pledge to never sign any trade agreement that hurts our workers, or that diminishes our freedom and independence. . . . Reducing taxes will cause new companies and new jobs to come roaring back into our country.[54]

Trump restated his promise to build a wall along the US-Mexico border and to ban immigrants from countries plagued by terrorism. As he had done throughout the campaign, Trump repeated his vow to repeal and replace the Affordable Care Act, or Obamacare. This federal program provided access to medical insurance for more than 22 million people, but Republicans strongly opposed it and had been seeking its repeal for years.

Trump assured listeners that his main motivation as president was to give a voice to the voiceless—those who, he said, had long been ignored by mainstream politicians. And he proclaimed that only he could accomplish this feat:

> I have joined the political arena so that the powerful can no longer beat up on people that cannot defend themselves. Nobody knows the system better than me, which is why I alone can fix it. . . . On January 21st of 2017, the day after I take the oath of office, Americans will finally wake up in a country where the laws of the United States are enforced.[55]

Curious Statements

After the convention Trump continued to campaign as he had during the primaries. He railed against the media, Muslims, and Mexican immigrants. And he continued to make statements that many Americans considered to be outrageous. In August, Trump repeatedly claimed that the president of the United States had founded ISIS. In one interview, conservative radio host Hugh Hewitt asked Trump to clarify this charge. Hewitt asked Trump if he meant that Obama's inaction in Syria had opened the way for the formation of ISIS. Trump said, "No, I meant he's the founder of ISIS. I do. He was the most valuable player. I give him the most valuable player award. I give her, too, by the way, Hillary Clinton."[56]

Although many politicians make questionable statements, no presidential candidate in modern times ever spoke like Trump. And many were alarmed by Trump's information sources. One of Trump's closest political advisers, Steve Bannon, was chief executive officer of the website Breitbart News Network. The site is known for promoting so-called alternative right, or alt-right, views. The ideology behind these views, according to the Associated Press, is a mix of racism, white nationalism, and populism. Breitbart has used offensive and racist terms in reference to Jews, African Americans, Muslims, women, and gay and transgender people. Trump has disavowed the so-called alt-right movement and defended Bannon, saying he believes he is neither racist nor anti-Semitic.

Conspiracy theorist Alex Jones was another Trump source. Jones produces a radio program, *The Alex Jones Show,* and a related website called Infowars. Jones was the source of a much-repeated claim that Democrats were bringing millions of undocumented immigrants to the polls in November to vote for Clinton. Jones also claimed that

> "I have joined the political arena so that the powerful can no longer beat up on people that cannot defend themselves. Nobody knows the system better than me, which is why I alone can fix it."[55]
>
> — Donald Trump

individual Democrats in big cities would return to the polls to vote ten times or more. Within days, Trump began repeating these statements in his campaign speeches. This even surprised Jones, who told his listeners, "It is surreal to talk about issues here on air, and then word-for-word hear Trump say it two days later."[57]

A Huge Upset

The unprecedented negativity of the long campaign was taking its toll on average Americans. An October poll taken by the American Psychological Association showed that 52 percent of American adults were stressed out by the election; Republicans and Democrats were equally likely to feel the election was a significant source of anxiety. Therapist Steven Stosny explained how the stress impacted millions of Americans: "It feels like irritability and resentment, covering up anxiety and a sense of powerlessness. It creates a tendency to blame, oversimplify and devalue other perspectives."[58]

> "It is surreal to talk about issues here on air, and then word-for-word hear Trump say it two days later."[57]
>
> — Alex Jones, radio host and conspiracy theorist

As the November 8 election neared, almost every poll showed Clinton beating Trump by about 2 percentage points. But on election night, as exit polls and vote tallies began filtering in, it became clear that Trump had staged a huge upset. On November 9, at 3:00 a.m. Eastern time, Trump had secured 270 electoral votes, enough to make him president-elect of the United States. The following morning Clinton gave a tearful concession speech: "I know how disappointed you feel because I feel it too, and so do tens of millions of Americans who invested their hopes and dreams in this effort. . . . Our campaign was never about one person or even one election, it was about the country we love and about building an America that's hopeful, inclusive and big-hearted."[59]

Trump's victory sounded a similar tone. He praised Clinton for fighting hard in the campaign and promised to be a president to Americans of all races, religions, backgrounds, and beliefs:

Working together, we will begin the urgent task of rebuilding our nation and renewing the American dream. I've spent my entire life in business, looking at the untapped potential in projects and in people all over the world. That is now what I want to do for our country. Tremendous potential. . . . It is going to be a beautiful thing. Every single American will have the opportunity to realize his or her fullest potential.[60]

Winning the Electoral College

Trump was now slated to become the forty-fifth president of the United States. But when all the vote totals were officially counted and certified

The Russian Hacking Controversy

The 2016 presidential election was unprecedented in many ways, but perhaps the most bizarre aspect concerned Russia's interference in the election. According to a January 2017 report by the US Intelligence Community (USIC), hackers acting under orders of Russian president Vladimir Putin stole private e-mails from servers owned by the Democratic National Committee, the governing body of the Democratic Party. The USIC, which consists of sixteen military and civilian intelligence agencies, stated that

> Russia's goals were to undermine public faith in the US democratic process, denigrate Secretary Clinton, and harm her electability and potential presidency. We further assess Putin and the Russian Government . . . aspired to help President-elect Trump's election chances when possible by discrediting Secretary Clinton and publicly contrasting her unfavorably to him.

Trump's immediate reaction, communicated via Twitter, was to attack US intelligence agencies for releasing the report. He claimed that reports about the Russian interference were meant to detract from the legitimacy of his election. Trump also stated his belief that it was impossible to know who did the hacking. He said it could have been anyone from the Chinese government to a fourteen-year-old in his parent's basement. On January 11, 2017—nine days before his inauguration—Trump finally conceded that Russia probably meddled in the election.

Quoted in Jessica Schulberg, "Intelligence Report Concludes That Vladimir Putin Intervened in US Election to Help Donald Trump Win," *Huffington Post*, January 6, 2017. www.huffingtonpost.com.

several weeks after the election, the tally showed that Clinton had actually won the popular vote. She received 65.8 million votes compared to Trump's 62.9 million.

Although Clinton had beaten Trump by 2.9 million votes, American presidents are not elected by popular vote. Presidents are picked by the electoral college, established in Article Two of the US Constitution. The electoral college consists of 538 electors from fifty states and the District of Columbia. Each state has a specific number of electoral votes based on the number of congressional districts within the state. California, with 55 congressional representatives, has 55 electoral votes. Nebraska, with 5 congressional representatives, has 5 electoral votes. The candidate who wins a majority of the popular vote in an individual state receives that state's electoral votes. On the basis of vote totals in every state, Trump received 306 electoral votes compared to 232 for Clinton.

Trump was only the fifth person in American history to lose the popular vote but win the presidency through the electoral college. The last time was in 2000 when George W. Bush lost the popular vote by around half a million votes to Al Gore but won the presidency because he had more electoral votes. Trump's win in the electoral college—and Clinton's higher numbers in the popular vote—reignited debate over the role of the electoral college in modern presidential campaigns. At one time Trump had declared the electoral college a disaster for democracy, but after his victory he tweeted a different message: "The Electoral College is actually genius in that it brings all states, including the smaller ones, into play."[61]

Even though he had won the presidency, Trump was not pleased with losing the popular vote. He claimed that Clinton's 2.9 million margin was the result of illegal votes. He tweeted, "[There was] serious voter fraud in Virginia, New Hampshire, and California."[62] This claim was debunked by numerous state and national officials, but the president-elect continued to tweet it—and many of his supporters continued to believe it.

The Inauguration

On January 20, 2017 Donald Trump was sworn in as the forty-fifth president of the United States. At the age of seventy, Trump was the oldest president to begin a first term. During his sixteen-minute inaugural speech, Trump hewed to the themes that brought him to this historic day. He described a nation reeling from unemployment, crime, drug abuse, and poverty while attacking the political establishment of both parties: "Washington flourished—but the people did not share in its wealth. Politicians prospered—but the jobs left, and the factories closed. . . . The wealth of our middle class has been ripped from their homes and then redistributed across the entire world." Trump outlined his plans to put America first: "Every decision on trade, on taxes, on immigration, on foreign affairs, will be made to benefit American workers and American families."[63] Trump called for national unity, saying there is no room for prejudice in the United States.

Even as the new president spoke, millions of people across the country and around the globe were planning demonstrations for the next day. Although not intended as a protest against Trump specifically, the demonstrations highlighted concerns about the new president's views and policies—and the statements he made during and after the campaign—in connection with women, immigrants, African Americans, Muslims, the environment, and more. The marches were all associated with the Women's March on Washington, which, according to

Protesters fill the streets of downtown Los Angeles on January 21, 2017, as part of a series of marches called the Women's March. Millions of marchers across the nation and around the world highlighted their concerns about the new president's policies and statements.

the *New York Times*, attracted around 470,000 people in Washington, DC, alone. Affiliated demonstrations called Sister Marches were held in more than 650 cities, large and small. These included New York City; Los Angeles; Austin, Texas; Oklahoma City; Ogden, Utah; and Fairbanks, Alaska. Researchers at the University of Connecticut estimated that at least 3.3 million people in the United States participated in the Women's March. Millions more marched in cities around the

Donald Trump's Inauguration Speech

After Trump took the oath of office to become the forty-fifth president of the United States, he gave a speech that reflected his main campaign theme—putting Americans first. The speech is excerpted below:

> I will fight for you with every breath in my body—and I will never, ever let you down.
>
> America will start winning again, winning like never before.
>
> We will bring back our jobs. We will bring back our borders. We will bring back our wealth. And we will bring back our dreams.
>
> We will build new roads, and highways, and bridges, and airports, and tunnels, and railways all across our wonderful nation.
>
> We will get our people off of welfare and back to work—rebuilding our country with American hands and American labor.
>
> We will follow two simple rules: Buy American and hire American.
>
> We will seek friendship and goodwill with the nations of the world—but we do so with the understanding that it is the right of all nations to put their own interests first.
>
> We do not seek to impose our way of life on anyone, but rather to let it shine as an example for everyone to follow. . . .
>
> So to all Americans, in every city near and far, small and large, from mountain to mountain, and from ocean to ocean, hear these words:
>
> You will never be ignored again.
>
> Your voice, your hopes, and your dreams will define our American destiny. And your courage and goodness and love will forever guide us along the way.

Quoted in CNN, "Inaugural Address: Trump's Full Speech," January 20, 2017. www.cnn.com.

President Donald Trump signs executive orders in the White House Oval Office just days after his inauguration.

world, including Paris, Berlin, London, Tokyo, Mexico City, and New Delhi, India.

Even though most Americans did not march in the streets, Trump's approval rating hit a new low as he was sworn in as president. A Fox News poll showed that 37 percent of Americans approved of Trump. This made him the most unpopular incoming president since the polling organizations began keeping track in 1952. By comparison, 80 percent approved of Obama when he was first inaugurated in 2008.

Proud, Safe, and Great

Trump proved to be the most surprising presidential candidate in American history. He began his career as a shrewd developer and used his business instincts to become an international celebrity. When he entered the race for president, he found ways to use the power of television, social media, and the Internet better than any of his competitors.

He built on his appeal as a flashy reality television star and wealthy global showman. He won over voters who were tired of politics as usual and angry about the changes taking place around them by speaking his mind—regardless of whom he offended or whether his comments fit the facts.

Donald Trump's victory highlighted the political divisions in America that had been growing for years. Trump supporters hope he will shake up Washington, DC, and improve their lives. Opponents remain fearful of what the unpredictable candidate might do as president. Only time will tell whether Trump will unite the country or divide it further. Trump, however, has no doubt about what he hopes to accomplish. As he stated in his inaugural address: "We will make America strong again. We will make America wealthy again. We will make America proud again. We will make America safe again. And yes, together, we will make America great again."[64]

Source Notes

Introduction: A Bet That Paid Off

1. Gwenda Blair, *The Trumps: Three Generations of Builders and a Presidential Candidate.* New York: Simon & Schuster, 2015, p. 12.
2. Quoted in *Time* staff, "Here's Donald Trump's Presidential Announcement Speech," *Time,* June 16, 2015. http://time.com.
3. Chris Cillizza, "Why No One Should Take Donald Trump Seriously, in One Very Simple Chart," *Washington Post,* June 17, 2015. www.washingtonpost.com.
4. Viet Thanh Nguyen, "Listen to Radicals, Artists," *Los Angeles Times,* November 20, 2016, p. F10.

Chapter 1: Born Into a Wealthy Family

5. Quoted in Politico staff, "Full Text: Donald Trump 2016 RNC Draft Speech Transcript," Politico, July 21, 2016. www.politico.com.
6. Jason Horowitz, "Fred Trump Taught His Son the Essentials of Showboating Self-Promotion," *New York Times,* August 12, 2016. www.nytimes.com.
7. Quoted in Paul Schwartzman and Michael E. Miller, "Confident. Incorrigible. Bully: Little Donny Was a Lot Like Candidate Donald Trump," *Washington Post,* June 22, 2016. www.washingtonpost.com.
8. Donald Trump and Tony Schwartz, *Trump: The Art of the Deal.* New York: Ballantine Books, 1987, pp. 71–72.
9. Trump and Schwartz, *Trump,* pp. 72–73.
10. Trump and Schwartz, *Trump,* p. 81.
11. Trump and Schwartz, *Trump,* p. 83.
12. Quoted in Michael Kranish and Marc Fisher, *Trump Revealed: An American Journey of Ambition, Ego, Money, and Power.* New York: Simon & Schuster, 2016, p. 55.

13. Quoted in Morris Kaplan, "US Accuses Major Landlord of Bias," *New York Times,* October 16, 1973. www.nytimes.com.

14. Quoted in David W. Dunlap, "1973: Meet Donald Trump," *New York Times*, July 30, 2015. www.nytimes.com.

Chapter 2: Winning and Losing in Business

15. Prachi Gupta, "6 Things You Need to Know About Donald Trump's First Wife, Ivana," *Cosmopolitan*, April 8, 2016. www.cosmopolitan .com.

16. Trump and Schwartz, *Trump,* p. 121.

17. Quoted in Kranish and Fisher, *Trump Revealed,* p. 82.

18. Trump and Schwartz, *Trump,* p. 107.

19. Quoted in Michael D'Antonio, "Donald Trump Isn't Crazy," CNN, August 2, 2016. www.cnn.com.

20. Quoted in Kranish and Fisher, *Trump Revealed,* p. 96.

21. Trump and Schwartz, *Trump,* p. 47.

22. Quoted in Blair, *The Trumps,* p. 145.

23. Quoted in Chris Isidore, "Everything You Want to Know About Donald Trump's Bankruptcies," CNN, August 21, 2015. http:// money.cnn.com.

24. Quoted in Russ Buettner and Charles V. Bagli, "How Donald Trump Bankrupted His Atlantic City Casinos, but Still Earned Millions," *New York Times*, June 11, 2016. www.nytimes.com.

Chapter 3: Celebrity and Politics

25. Quoted in Lily Rothman, "Donald Trump's Concern About Nuclear Weapons Dates Back Decades," *Time*, September 26, 2016. http://time.com.

26. Kranish and Fisher, *Trump Revealed,* p. 153.

27. Quoted in Kranish and Fisher, *Trump Revealed,* p. 166.

28. Quoted in Andrew Kaczynski, Chris Massie, and Nate McDermott, "Donald Trump to Howard Stern: It's Okay to Call My Daughter a 'Piece of Ass,'" CNN, October 9, 2016. www.cnn.com.

29. Quoted in Kranish and Fisher, *Trump Revealed,* p. 167.

30. Quoted in *Larry King Live,* "Encore Presentation: Interview with 'The Apprentice' Host Donald Trump," CNN, April 18, 2004. www.cnn.com.

31. Quoted in Christopher Massie, "Trump on Donating to Democrats: As a Business Person, 'You're Gonna Need Things from Everybody," BuzzFeed News, June 22, 2015. www.buzzfeed.com.

32. Quoted in Frank Camp, "Before Trump Was Slamming President Obama, He Was Giving Him High Praise in 2009," *Independent Journal Review*, January 6, 2016. http://ijr.com.

33. Jess Henig, "Born in the U.S.A.," FactCheck.org, August 21, 2008. www.factcheck.org.

34. Quoted in Gregory Krieg, "14 of Trump's Most Outrageous 'Birther' Claims—Half from After 2011," CNN, September 16, 2016. www.cnn.com.

35. Quoted in Krieg, "14 of Trump's Most Outrageous 'Birther' Claims."

36. Quoted in Alex Eichler, "Was the Birther Movement Always About Race?," *Atlantic*, April 28, 2011. www.theatlantic.com.

37. Quoted in Gregory Kreig, "Sound Familiar? Trump Called 2012 Vote a 'Total Sham,'" CNN, October 20, 2016. www.cnn.com.

38. Quoted in Meghan Keneally, "Donald Trump's History of Raising Birther Questions About President Obama," ABC News, September 18, 2015. http://abcnews.go.com.

Chapter 4: An Unconventional Candidate

39. Quoted in Olivia Goldhill, "Five Reality TV Show Strategies Donald Trump Has Used Throughout His Campaign," Quartz, November 6, 2016. https://qz.com.

40. Quoted in *Time* staff, "Here's Donald Trump's Presidential Announcement Speech."

41. Quoted in *Time* staff, "Here's Donald Trump's Presidential Announcement Speech."

42. Quoted in *Time* staff, "Here's Donald Trump's Presidential Announcement Speech."

43. Kranish and Fisher, *Trump Revealed,* p. 309.

44. Quoted in Maeve Reston, "No One Eclipses Donald Trump at GOP Debate," CNN, August 7, 2015. www.cnn.com.

45. Seth Stevenson, "A Week on the Trail with the 'Disgusting Reporters' Covering Donald Trump," *Slate*, March 20, 2016. www.slate.com.

46. Quoted in Stephen M. Lepore, "A Guide to Trump's Insults of Every 2016 Candidate," *New York Daily News*, September 10, 2015. www.nydailynews.com.

47. Tom Krattenmaker, "The Republican Race Is a Reality Show," *Huffington Post,* January 26, 2016. www.huffingtonpost.com.

48. Quoted in Jeremy Diamond, "Trump: I Could 'Shoot Somebody and I Wouldn't Lose Voters,'" CNN, January 24, 2016. www.cnn.com.

49. Quoted in German Lopez, "Don't Believe Donald Trump Has Incited Violence at Rallies? Watch This Video," Vox, March 12, 2016. www.vox.com.

50. David Wong, "How Half of America Lost Its F**king Mind," *Cracked*, October 12, 2016. www.cracked.com.

Chapter 5: Trump Wins

51. Quoted in Dan Roberts, Ben Jacobs, and Sabrina Siddiqui, "Donald Trump Threatens to Jail Hillary Clinton in Second Presidential Debate," *Guardian* (Manchester, UK), October 10, 2016. www.theguardian.com.

52. Ezra Klein, "Understanding Hillary," Vox, July 11, 2016. www.vox.com.

53. Quoted in Politico staff, "Donald Trump 2016 RNC Draft Speech Transcript," Politico, July 21, 2016. www.politico.com.

54. Quoted in Politico staff, "Donald Trump 2016 RNC Draft Speech Transcript."

55. Quoted in Politico staff, "Donald Trump 2016 RNC Draft Speech Transcript."

56. Quoted in Tal Kopan, "Donald Trump: I Mean That Obama Founded ISIS, Literally," CNN, August 12, 2016. www.cnn.com.

57. Quoted in Tim Murphy, "How Donald Trump Became Conspiracy Theorist in Chief," *Mother Jones*, November/December 2016. www.motherjones.com.

58. Quoted in Colby Itkowitz, "Feeling Anxious Ahead of the Debate? Here's How to Cope with 'Election Stress Disorder,'" *Washington Post*, September 26, 2016. www.washingtonpost.com.

59. Quoted in CNN, "Hillary Clinton's Concession Speech," November 9, 2016. www.cnn.com.

60. Quoted in CNN staff, "Here's the Full Text of Donald Trump's Victory Speech," CNN, November 9, 2016. www.cnn.com.

61. Quoted in Glenn Kessler, "Trump's Flip-Flop on the Electoral College: From 'Disaster' to 'Genius,'" *Washington Post*, November 15, 2016. www.washingtonpost.com.

62. Quoted in Tom LoBianco, "Trump Falsely Claims 'Millions of People Who Voted Illegally' Cost Him Popular Vote," CNN, November 28, 2016. www.cnn.com.

63. Quoted in CNN, "Inaugural Address: Trump's Full Speech," January 20, 2017. www.cnn.com.

64. Quoted in CNN, "Inaugural Address."

Important Events in the Life of Donald Trump

1946
Donald John Trump is born on June 14 in New York City.

1970
Trump begins working with his father developing real estate in Queens and Brooklyn.

1977
Donald Trump marries Ivana Zelnicekova.

1980
Trump's first New York City development, the Grand Hyatt Hotel, opens.

1983
Trump Tower opens on Fifth Avenue in Manhattan.

1984
Trump opens Harrah's at Trump Plaza in Atlantic City, New Jersey.

1987
Trump's best-selling book, *Trump: The Art of the Deal,* is published.

1991

One of Trump's casinos is forced into bankruptcy.

1992

Two more of Trump's casinos file for bankruptcy.

1993

Trump marries Marla Maples.

1996

Trump purchases the Miss Universe, Miss USA, and Miss Teen USA pageants.

2004

The reality show *The Apprentice,* with Trump as host, debuts on NBC.

2005

Trump marries Melania Knauss.

2009

Trump Entertainment Resorts declares bankruptcy.

2011

Trump becomes the loudest voice in the birther movement, promoting the idea that President Barack Obama was born in Kenya.

2015

Trump announces his intention to run for president in a June speech at Trump Tower in New York.

2016

Trump wins the presidential election.

2017

Trump is sworn in as the forty-fifth president of the United States.

For Further Research

Books

Craig E. Blohm, *Hillary Clinton*. San Diego: ReferencePoint, 2016.

A.R. Carser, *Donald Trump: 45th US President*. Minneapolis: ABDO, 2017.

Lisa A Crayton, *Recession: What It Is and How It Works*. New York: Enslow, 2016.

Jennifer Fandel, *Democracy*. Mankato, MN: Creative Paperbacks, 2017.

Barbara Krasner, *A Timeline of Presidential Elections*. Mankato, MN: Capstone, 2016.

Tara Ross, *We Elect a President: The Story of Our Electoral College*. Ashland, OH: Colonial, 2016.

Jill Sherman, *Donald Trump: Outspoken Personality and President*. Minneapolis: Lerner, 2017.

Internet Sources

National Archives and Records Administration, "What Is the Electoral College?," 2016. www.archives.gov/federal-register/electoral-college/about .html.

Politico staff, "Donald Trump 2016 RNC Draft Speech Transcript," Politico, July 21, 2016. www.politico.com/story/2016/07/full-tran script-donald-trump-nomination-acceptance-speech-at-rnc-225974.

Time staff, "Here's Donald Trump's Presidential Announcement Speech," *Time*, June 16, 2015. http://time.com/3923128/donald-trump -announcement-speech.

Jerry Useem, "What Does Donald Trump Really Want?," *Fortune,* April 3, 2000. http://fortune.com/2000/04/03/what-does-donald-trump -really-want.

Websites

Donald J. Trump for President (www.donaldjtrump.com). Donald Trump's official 2016 presidential campaign website with press releases, policy positions, and other information.

Donald Trump News (http://abcnews.go.com/topics/news/donald -trump.htm). The latest news and in-depth coverage of Trump by ABC News with headlines, photos, and videos.

Donald Trump's File (www.politifact.com/personalities/donald-trump). The nonpartisan website PolitiFact fact-checks Trump's statements and keeps a running tally on how many are true, mostly true, false, and "Pants on Fire," or totally false.

2016 Election Results (www.cnn.com/election/results). This CNN website provides information about the states won by each candidate along with popular vote totals and information about congressional races.

Index

Picture Credits

Cover: Associated Press

6: James Messerschmidt/Polaris/Newscom

9: Associated Press

11: Piero Oliosi/Polaris/Newscom

14: Splash News/Newscom

16: Vietnam War Protest. Demonstrators in Washington, DC, sitting-in in protest of the Vietnam War, 21 May 1972/Bridgeman Images

23: Associated Press

25: USA, New York City, Manhattan, Trump Tower/Dorling Kindersley/ UIG/Bridgeman Images

28: PhotoLink/Newscom

32: Associated Press

34: Associated Press

40: Brendan McDermit/Reuters/Newscom

45: Associated Press

49: Carlos Barria/Reuters/Newscom

54: Depositphotos/Gino's Photos

57: Kevin Dietsch/UPI/Newscom

63: Associated Press

65: Associated Press